T0011384

SUPER
SURPRISING
TRiViA
ABOUT
the MIDDLE
AGES

by Megan Cooley Peterson

CAPSTONE PRESS
a capstone imprint

Spark is published by Capstone Press, an imprint of Capstone
1710 Roe Crest Drive, North Mankato, Minnesota 56003
capstonepub.com

Copyright © 2024 by Capstone. All rights reserved. No part of this
publication may be reproduced in whole or in part, or stored in a retrieval
system, or transmitted in any form or by any means, electronic, mechanical,
photocopying, recording, or otherwise, without written permission of the
publisher.

Library of Congress Cataloging-in-Publication Data is available on the
Library of Congress website.
ISBN: 9781669064831 (hardcover)
ISBN: 9781669071730 (paperback)
ISBN: 9781669064862 (ebook PDF)

Summary: Do you love European history? Have you imagined what it
would be like to live in a castle among royalty and knights? From odd
recipes, disgusting toilet trivia, and bizarre medical treatments, get the
inside scoop about what life was really like in the Middle Ages in this
amazing book of Middle Ages trivia.

Editorial Credits
Editor: Mandy Robbins; Designer: Heidi Thompson; Media Researcher:
Jo Miller; Production Specialist: Tori Abraham

Image Credits
Alamy: Album, 29, Antiqua Print Gallery, 16, Chronicle, 8, 13 (bottom),
FALKENSTEINFOTO, 21, Heritage Image Partnership Ltd, 13 (top),
Historical Images Archive, 17, Lebrecht Music & Arts, 5, North Wind Picture
Archives, 9 (top), Science History Images, 23; Getty Images: duncan1890,
Cover (bottom left), 28, Henry Guttmann Collection, 24, Nastasic, 26,
SCIEPRO, 19 (bottom), ZU_09, 27; Shutterstock: AMC Photography, Cover
(top left), Anna_Huchak, 19 (top), BY-_-BY, Cover (top right), Eric Isselee,
Cover (bottom right), 14, FineShine, 9 (bottom), Frank Wagner, 15, Mikulas
P, 22, photomaster, 7 (right), Ratikova, 7 (left), talseN, 25, Tatiana_Pink, 18,
Yasonya, 20, zcw, 10 (bottom); Superstock: imageBROKER/Christian Handl,
12; TopFoto, 10 (top), Heritage-Images, 6, 11

All internet sites appearing in back matter were available and accurate when
this book was sent to press.

Printed and bound in the USA. 5626

TABLE OF CONTENTS

Words in **bold** are in the glossary.

THE MIND-BLOWING MIDDLE AGES

The Middle Ages were a smelly, busy time in Europe. They lasted from about the year 500 to 1500. Life was very different back then. No one had toothbrushes or smartphones. People ate strange foods. Knights needed help getting dressed. Want to learn some fun facts about the Middle Ages? Read on!

Tending fields by hand was part of daily life in the Middle Ages.

5

THEY ATE WHAT?

Food was different in the Middle Ages. Cats were sometimes on the menu—but not their heads. Eating a cat's head was bad luck.

Chefs for fancy dinners served swan and peacock. After roasting the birds, they added back the feathers.

Some pies had live songbirds inside them. But people didn't eat the birds. It was just for fun.

Pickled boar's head was a popular dish too. A boar is a type of pig.

Rich people ate whale and **porpoise** tongues.

Most people baked their bread in a town oven. Everyone shared this oven. Only rich people had their own ovens.

People ate animal organs such as brains and intestines. No part of the animal went to waste.

People ate with their hands. They didn't have forks yet. But guests did bring their own knives for cutting.

WHERE DID THE WASTE GO?

Flush toilets hadn't been invented yet. People used wood or stone with a hole cut into it.

Waste dropped from the hole into a **cesspit**. Workers called gong farmers cleaned them out.

In some places, waste fell into a river or stream. Those rivers and streams were also used for drinking water. Yuck!

Cities collected urine from public toilets. The pee was used to remove oils from sheep wool. The wool could then be made into cloth.

Small bump-outs in a castle's tower walls held toilets. Waste dropped into a moat or river below.

Soldiers climbed up stinky sewer shafts to break into enemy castles.

Pipes in London, England, were made of wood in the 1100s. Water flowed into the city through hollowed-out tree trunks.

London, England, in the Middle Ages

Most streets were packed dirt. Water and waste flowed through the gutters next to the road. Animals pooped right on the street.

THE SMELLY, PAINFUL MIDDLE AGES

People bathed about once a week in the Middle Ages.

People made homemade soap out of animal fat and ashes.

Picking **lice** off one another was a normal part of staying clean.

In the Middle Ages, people didn't brush their teeth. They wiped their teeth with rags. They chewed on mint leaves to freshen their breath.

Dentists poured acid into **cavities**. The acid killed the nerve. It stopped the pain. It also ruined the tooth.

Have a toothache in the Middle Ages? Put some raven poop on it! Lots of people did. But it didn't actually help.

Doctors had people carry containers of good-smelling spices. They thought good smells stopped diseases from spreading.

Doctors thought removing "bad blood" from sick people was healing. During **bloodletting,** they cut into a patient's **vein**. This could do more harm than good.

Barber-surgeons performed bloodletting in between shaves and haircuts.

Doctors smelled and touched their patients' blood to make a **diagnosis**. They even tasted it!

Doctors studied the color of urine. Blue, black, and red were considered very bad.

Doctors used pig poop to stop nosebleeds. They put it on their patients' noses. But this stinky cure didn't work.

GOING INTO BATTLE

Knights and their horses wore armor into battle. Armor was made of metal, cloth, leather, metal rings, or animal horns.

Full plate armor was made of metal.

It protected against cuts and broken bones.

Some knights wore chain mail. Tiny metal rings were joined together to create it. Swords couldn't cut through mail. But they could still break bones.

A **squire** helped a knight put on his armor. It could take a squire up to a half hour to dress a knight.

Knights were sometimes buried with their swords.

Longbowmen were a type of knight.

They could fire 12 arrows a minute.

Glossary

bloodletting (BLUHD-lett-ing)—medical treatment for cleansing the blood, by making the patient bleed

cavity (KA-vuh-tee)—a hole in a tooth caused by decay

cesspit (SESS-pit)—pit for storing sewage and, sometimes, other waste

diagnosis (dy-ig-NOH-suhs)—finding a cause for a problem or illness

lice (LYSE)—bloodsucking insects that live on humans and other mammals

longbowman (LAWNG-boh-man)—a knight who fired a longbow; a longbow is weapon based on the bow and arrow

pickled (PIH-kuhld)—when food is preserved in a liquid that makes it last longer

porpoise (por-PUHS)—a small-toothed whale with a rounded head and short, blunt snout

squire (SKWIRE)—a young nobleman who served as an attendant to a knight

vein (VAYN)—a blood vessel that carries blood back to the heart

Read More

Burgan, Michael. *The Middle Ages*. Washington, D.C.: National Geographic Partners, LLC, 2023.

Fabiny, Sarah. *What Are Castles and Knights?* New York: Penguin Workshop, 2022.

Hansen, Grace. *History's Ancient and Medieval Secrets*. Minneapolis: DiscoverRoo, an imprint of Pop!, 2023.

Internet Sites

DK Find Out!: Castles
dkfindout.com/us/history/castles/

Medieval Medicine Facts for Kids
historyforkids.org/medieval-medicine/

Middle Ages for Kids: Daily Life
ducksters.com/history/middle_ages/daily_life_in_the_middle_ages.php

Index

About the Author

Megan Cooley Peterson is a children's book author and editor. When not writing, Megan enjoys movies, books, and all things Halloween. She lives in Minnesota with her husband and daughter.